A Conjoined Book:

AFTERMATH ❈ *Become Tree, Become Bird*

ALSO BY KARLA KELSEY

Knowledge, Forms, the Aviary
Ahsahta, 2006

Iteration Nets
Ahsahta, 2010

A CONJOINED BOOK:

AFTERMATH ❋ *Become Tree, Become Bird*

KARLA KELSEY

OMNIDAWN PUBLISHING
RICHMOND, CALIFORNIA
2014

Cover art by Ashley Lamb: *Moss*, collage, 9.5" x 7.5," 2013.
(http://ashleyklamb.com/)
&
Black seamless pattern, vector silhouette
by Natykach Nataliia/Shutterstock

Book cover & interior design by Cassandra Smith

Offset printed in the United States
by Edwards Brothers Malloy, Ann Arbor, Michigan
on 55# Enviro Natural 100/% Recycled 100% PCW
Acid Free Archival Quality FSC Certified Paper
with Rainbow FSC Certified Colored End Papers

Library of Congress Cataloging-in-Publication Data

Kelsey, Karla.
[Poems. Selections]
A conjoined book : Aftermath : Become tree, become bird / Karla Kelsey.
    pages cm
ISBN 978-1-890650-94-0 (Trade Paperback : alk. paper)
I. Title.
PS3611.E473A6 2014
811'.6--dc23

                                                            2013045790

Published by Omnidawn Publishing, Richmond, California
www.omnidawn.com   (510) 237-5472   (800) 792-4957
            10 9 8 7 6 5 4 3 2 1
            ISBN: 978-1-890650-94-0

TABLE OF CONTENTS

AFTERMATH

"Like a ribbon of weed I am flung far every time the door opens. The wave breaks. I am the foam that sweeps & fills the uttermost rims of the rocks with whiteness; I am also a girl, here in this room."

Virginia Woolf, *The Waves*

I awake mid-
thought & feeling

the bed sheets taut
I lily over-

rained & burgeoning. This season

of metal left to rust,
the house closed up

& emptying down

the gravel walk

Facets shine off the river & the character appears in her robe stitched with peacock eyes, skilled in grasping what her mother meant when she said now this is your life & so you live it. But what is it that she's looking for, miming the gesture of a pair of doves gone home to the cote

The lost more likely
to be found in this

field fertilized & then gone
to the slatted-board wind
& a pearling of eye to eye

a bridge repeatedly painted.
As if decay meant becoming one

with songs of the hounding hour

her room saturate with tree-shadow with the lamppost its globe swanning out.
Moment by moment her eye sticks, teetering "here," asking questions to the
window aslant with geese. In discouragement of dried lilac clinging to its stalk,
the radio alarm, the pouring

Your arms air & sail & in this
you deal seed to the irises compressed

the iron-wrought corner,
small garden. But we were
entering the season of hothouse roses

& cracked jars, the turned
& purchased error
meaning the seed did rot, effort dissolved

in the firebreak divide
of pasture from pasture

she conceives of herself as a memory, light-threadings of fireworks reflected off
windshields, reflected off the slow-moving river. But what would you prefer
to see layering the girl: image after image stalled into life? A rock shattering
concentric circles into the river's surface?

& so turning in departure the dock dipped & the world turned on its side
until months later I looked to the future of zinc set against rust, oscillation
& char seen
through a
claude-glass
with a green tint & whitecaps whipped by the current & breeze of if
I. But if I am in & through the window & the autumn storm walking
through blossom-bare lilac to crouch under the holly tree, departure
composed
in the view
from the dock drawn in nettle & air as inside the shelter of my body we
fall, particles of sand & salt among water-vented pollen dispersed by image
& breeze. This discord saturates with the seen-through-a-glass, with the
wait-in-the-doorway-until-you-recognize that your name is only a problem
under the
distance
of certain systems, constituting, reconstituting, the barn sinking back
into aspen, leaves gone to mulch as light shines on the boy walking
down the sidewalk singing *Mary, Mary, Mary,* an attempt as in my eyes
settle on lupine
& sage, ocean &
field. The dog
barks & a choir of swallows preamble the hunting season, the turn-turn,
the nape of your neck as you said *lilac*—chosen in the hothouse interior
of her rooms with the gesture of a well, a steeple to the left piercing sky.

Pastured.
Pressed

between the city &
the city.

What does this have to do with my half-birthed

sutured to
the lily, the slow
burn the

alley, the lily, the lily glassy in prim vases always.

The mind a
golden circuit attached
to the holly
tree to the
sun relief

folded land

vantage stamped.
Copper
steeples
roofs &
cotton wing lines
flapped out

to the force caught
in the flick
of his head.

Mark-mark &
holding &
unholding
are null

flick of his mane

possibility fraught
by the green found en-ached

like Latin. Like a star-dividing-cell-astral-full-blooming in
the terra satellite, the sea-aster, the tripolium-novae-angliae a
wilded white horse

& so fell within
the mineral lick
for what of this
scored wind
found bent in
day fields crying

land-wound
&
land-wound.

Trumpet vine to maple branch lashed. Finch following finch aft the stone wall. The granite statuette stowed away & the wooden door scrapes closed. & I

                                                    was your

Rose, your Lily, your Loralie dying over & over with the slow pause of an early silver screen, grass gone nickel, skin gone glycerin.

                                  & in the corner the shotgun
& the emptied urn, rusted urn, the lifting stone where pillbugs curl & hide as heavy in wet wool you leave the scene through the garden door.

                                          Under the rubric
of excuse is the story in which I was last in a lineage of hunters, the once-seasonal rain that wouldn't go.

Now it was autumn & the end of the year mistaken for mineraled dirt, the time of departure become worn. From the moon's quarter to its half, rains had fallen & all the hill streams ran in flood. As the piano performs scale after scale the piano becomes exception.

& then I was the character in bed dreaming of beetles seeping from the plane of sleep to thick woven sheets & the beach outside my window littered with bodies. Under my lids. Not a solar flare or the extended dahlias of summer, the metal flower petals shape to my nipples creating this death in the small course birth's drawn out to pierce, to bleed through night a celestial thief. Negating the synchronized floral patterns of bedspread & drapery, the TV radiates the weight of explosion. Heat invades the troposphere, structures fall in perfect circles, after 15 days a burn appears in the shape of the ampoule I pocketed over my left breast. Clay birds circle the room, the partitions feel thinner than they really are. Over my heart. & this repeats in the mind gone heavy-wild with wind as she & I ply the narrative out at acute angles, a hush fallen over the line of children following a tractor engraving red clay.

Yoke of horse. Yoke of iron. Each perception's entry into the stream
is granted through seed, through the far corner of the field called wing
                                                touching wing
this our land created by the cut-through of the river. For what the river's
                                                washed away
in thinned light is left to silt & half-submerged trees, little farms in the
overrunning. These patterns construct my frequent thoughts where
                                                the river pools
under maples that each year leaf to darker crimson & I write the names
of flowers connoting the island's burn, flame replacing swallowtail, life-
                                                long fidelity
                                                as the sun
                                                does this work
of water moved through hands a liquid ribbon. A mirror reflecting a doe
recently shot & stripped, I watch myself approach the abandoned dining
car, dirty mattress in the corner heaped of smashed glass & cutlery. Take
                                                my hand. Air
                                                become
                                                dove. Air
become land grown granite-heavy & plinth, the river wides & slows
                                                & as wind
                                                shifts through
rue anemone on the ridge a bleating called force pries in, field washing
away, hills bone & the mind bone, bank split apart by crossties &
                                                meadow rose.

In the painting
the sky is blue
& the sky
in this window
is salt. No
heads cast back

no eyes strung up
to light flicked
through holes punched
in black canvas
clutch of lilies
hidden. Stay

in the room
as if the clock
stopped trying to say
nettle lover, season
bloom. Or I wished

to proceed
with rapidity
clouds traversing
so quickly
our bodies
became amber.
Blotted-out stars.

Yesterday was salt drawn

toward sliver & compression.

The distance

holding sentences.

Afterimages:

The window bathed in blue & the window bathed in
tourmaline. How to approach a series of photographs
torn from event, a collection of wounded nexuses.
Evidence of antecedents, discontinuities between them
laboring under a continuous dawn.

A form of looking

into the present state of attrition

eliciting truth.

This way the glass eye calls up the glass hand.
The slope of the harrowed field

hobnail. Or cut.

Afterimages:

Dresses scattered along the interstate. Silk & calico. His
hand poised with a match. Denim & linen. The billboard
of a house over-layering a house, her lips become nettle.
A rift in the landscape of memory, even when she tapes
the images together. Even when she fast-forwards them
on a reel.

Away from

these frequent patterns of thought

the sun

the pen

increasingly estranged.

Afterimages:

The radio alarm playing forgive me this silence my
dresses are burning. He was a sun changing his costume
all over the room, ashes float into the air. In pictures his
face has gone blanched from scald from freeze. The car a
sun a chair that wouldn't that couldn't go.

(Winter wanted the day, quiet summons under split branches. Profuse. & the path out & she follows the along & along. This is what they called for. That narrowing. That walking split-sided the atoll studded this North Atlantic gyre meanders to repair. To clear the grand scope. Driven off. Riven, this unseasonable breeze dim unraveling juniper, her home marred in the rim of the marrow—

then followed his blue coat down the path & then running.)

Internal of bees, river-drawn through corridors of trees I might touch with the body gone fragile.

       & if I.

                But if I. & this another name for the road marked by cattle moved to sickness, lining the way to the city.

                         Thus this. & the future-impossibilities raftered to sky, your image become a small bird pushed to the mirror, flown away in the hour it was held in the same frame as my hand.

                                  &

so worked the winnow-fan in rhythm to acres listing in harvest. Called to the fulgent-arena, running our hands through the seed.

As the water of the two feeder streams of the lake was deep & swift, the answer rusts to wire. An erroring edge called blue into darkening night, jostling the rocks of the stream as it hurries us down to the sea. We term otherwise in alternate measure: this is not voluntary, we are embarked.

The barn sinks back into the ground leaving behind tractor frame & oil drum, the book describing the ceremony as a circling of harvest. Here the secret entails the girls' yellow ribbons waving away in air, the sallying forth of horses, dust gone blue in the crowd in the shake of naked aspen. Vantage captured by a slow shutter by too much light in the eye. As such, they make the land gold. As such, they make their village new & hold together one & one & one like the canyon undergoing a moment of weather. She stands by the split-rail & watches, catches a ride into town walks the street of closed shops their mottled buildings granite-heavy & plinth. They'll tremble, just as the skies will tremble, just as she will tremble in their wake as if she could become part of the saying done in the small church, a stitch of hands. Here a photograph of the telephone pole leaning towards the steeple. Here a photograph of the diner he recently left with the gesture of a well, if not for the water then for the asking. Two plates & a lipstick-rimmed glass. Just a moment ago she stood alone by the side of the road in an attempt of saying, an attempt as in her eyes settle on the field, cross-hatched. A small hurt blooming in the base of her spine.

Told among the dreaming
the clock stopped
& the sky a crystal
of car horns, salt
of scale, the air
solid juncture
around breath. Stay

in the room. I feel
the window as you say
the raw light of
a bare bulb, a lever.
Enter the world

night-guided thoughts
still finding their way
home. Feathers
are what I mean

by solace eliminated
the chart & the lens
so we guessed
at the heavens, nettles
under my tongue
replacing the lever of bloom.

If not for these slim moments fit between paving stones. If not for
the season of birds slinging these shallows withdrawn from glance
& yet felt, simultaneously, in the ribs. Manifest in battering my body's
warm center is a consequence of yellow light blooming after the rain
                                        stopped &
                                        I saw you
afraid, interior become measure, the pool given at oblique angle
to the mouth of ice as stubble fields fall back. The road to the steel-
pivoted bridge half-anchors in demi-release, in memory, eyes closed
                                        to the swans
                                        on the banks
of the frozen lake, the lake then heated & drained without question
in the manner sentiment welds to regret & we're asked to the cut
                                        in the rock,
                                        the pouring
                                        known to
some as God. He is a naked branch of the all-white tree, null shade
for the ground where the lily sleeps in-mirrored as the tree inside my
                                        lungs expands.
                                        Knotted, grown
every which-way & winning over gravity, icy branches extend the flow
of words, hands, eyes lifted over powerlines, the arum lily become sails
                                        of a white
                                        ship in a
                                        white sea.

Forcing the feathers off
a regression, a turning around
to stare blankly. Then calling on

the high noise I was thorned
to the first moment, & then.
& then gunned-

up the mirror, the error
silver-shocked went out, the way

to the dove gone new in the apse
for the second moment distills
redemption. I was

how thought connects

to inner pink, to caught
in suspense along the valley dormant

along the river
the figure made up & troubled

in the world. Its feathers flown.

If she could fall from these frequented patterns of thought there would be the field but not the *drawn to the field*. The gesture of memory represents moments of fixation as the sun goes down, though in another scenario this would be a fractional element of fiction: a cut glass bowl holding a clutch of robin's eggs, albumen & yolk blown out. A postcard from the west featuring a lone palm arced over a sunset-riddled sea. She reads the message in white vapor trails fading into sky. A trio of motorcycles roars by. Residing inside each system: yellow's accretion undergoes reaping until at last the air golds. The only other man in the room besides you sends out low musk, draws slow circles with his pen, a ballad under his breath. In this scenario she climbs to the top of the hill an hour before sundown, marking each degree of declension with increasingly darker shades of crimson. Farm & field & farm. Road & truck & river & road & at the edge of sight the sea. Calico. On to night, then, for the story shifts into the place where he no longer refers to our character as *she*. Traded for a different referent, for the slope of white shoulders, the nape of a neck, low voice whispering *lilac* as faraway I—for who else to inhabit her vacated place—walk to the far corner of the field.

Dust man, one-among-a-number-of-dust-men, do you or do you not create a new road when you drive down & down to the sea?

The real featured, made deliberately an object of intention.

& in such an object I tamp down your each success. Which they call cruel & glossy though they don't know the sparrow bone where you cried *there-flower-there-follower* with couched intentions meant to be expressive of dawn.

But when we make those acts & their objects the objects of our attention—touch in the violet-shaded hollow, touch in lilac or the jet did score the sky—we discover spaces between the moments of a sequence.

Or have you grown out of the pit in my eye & the red barn leaning back into ground?

Tightened to shores of swollen russet, wind picking up at dusk, trees planted & clouds gliding flat & slow, surrounding air entrained with description. A weather system. Only at first had it been a gentle breeze, stroking our surface to velvet. You see, the stakes are sometimes somewhat higher than I spy you in the crow field marking you a crow man, another sack of dust.

Yesterday has not forgotten.

Though if it could
what would happen to

each low musk
each degree of

feathers cover my eyes.

Our portrait in mirror or water.

Afterimages:

As in the catapult theory of ruin the forgotten ghosts
through to the present. A diner, denim & linen. Though
they sit across from each other she is miles & miles from
here. A clay cloud, vision enthundered, I describe & I
describe. This task of a Sunday: the park quiet the lake
quiet the swans all gone.

Papered.

To remember
the field. The gestural

element of

the room
under breath.

A switchgrass account of solitude.

Afterimages:

When apocalypse arrives, doves in the corners of my
eyes. Sequence scattered in sun-dazzle, yet perception
insists on pattern. Slashes of light become constellations
underveining clouds. Feathers bear the trace of migration.
To what faith the constancy of blossom & fall. To what
avail the lost locket found.

& the remainder

would not be the field but

what we are drawn to. Would be

the season flooded in amber.

Afterimages:

Eyes closed & ruby zigzagging the underlids. Eyes open
& in the foreground a wolf & the lake rust-gold. A
snapshot view of transition solidifies what is otherwise
flux. What otherwise loses itself in olive green, sage
green, fused to a leaf. Conceptions crystallize by satellite.

pyrite
exposed to
water &
air produces
sulfuric acid
& iron
contaminants

abandoned
mine drainage
pressing up
to the
river (the
lake a
rainless
flood)

runoff
dissolving
copper
lead
mercury into
the watertable

(the scald
you
filled me
with)

Urged by the ebb of petals riven up, a marked waiting given the boy on the bank,
given the waving good-bye & good-bye.
                                        A bleating force as the field washed
away. A blued whistle beholden to the next clear day, breath held & told to be
nice now as the pitch in the dried-out riverbed,
                                        confession come through the
labor of husking, the sound of tractors working far fields.
                                        But for the distance
you are mine under the rubric of method.
                                        But for the light siding buildings,
power lines cracking with it, the sound of standing dismantled at the heart of the
harrowed.

The lake deeply altered by the inrush of contaminants sweeping our weed forests &
swirled through crayfish holes & then creeping up six inches on the trunks of
bordering willows. The river a sidewalk the wheel a stone & we heard that the
swans on the lake had been shot.

Blank forehead of asking the question to the room & an answer
in the bolt of a picture, a red horse sunk deep into deeper red, as
                                                    the earth
                                                    was red
                                                    there. &
there I blanched into aspen & window-split light, an afternoon V
                                                    mosaic-
                                                    worked
into plane tree, hush, bird egg cradled in the hollow of my hand
as song cries out from the pace of geese & memory of bees filling
air. Pictured in a wavering voice, in the watery voice of sirens called
                                                    through
                                                    an account
of solitude. Wrapped in torn blankets & rough sheets *I've seen between*
myself & myself writing stitched into eiderdown densed with breath
                                                    & so
infused with the chorused sun, melody dying out as dust blues
the crowd swaying like a canyon undergoing a moment of weather.
                                                    Slow &
                                                    strange we're
pulled south through blurred streets, getting out of our car to wander
the metal & salt of accident & shore. To come here bare or wrapped
in linen, the moment held in our bones as ash-light falls over the worried
                                                    edge of water
                                                    meeting sky.

A collection of wounded
nexuses, antecedents, hollows

for hollowed arms. & the red
torn from my dress from the

trees. & the blue torn from

the wind as a banner as a singular
moment stalled in yellow

banks covered over
with the lightest
of frost. & so gone

to the river & able
for this moment

to have been what was lost.

She was salt & abstract & he was zinc set against rust.
In this possibility there is a house on stilts & when the
river floods he plays piano she rocks the cradle the baby
cries. Earth & air over water. Or she saw the trading
of the future for this present state of attrition, no river
house, no baby, no watery tune. Subsumed. In the
path drawn towards oscillation & char, resignation in
abandoned arc, her perception yoked to horse & bone
of boat eliciting truth, his silver heat. & in being true
the texture of the moment turns to nettle & wood,
the stilts rotted under & the house fallen down. The
babydoll floated half-way to the sea. Through all of this
we'll stand at the edge of a far shore, carved in white.
Here she'll grow into an account of solitude versus her
portrait in mirror or water. More fascinating for its
warp, its hurrying on without her.

(Brokered through layers she remains cut at right angles to the sun. They move to the right of the tree to view the river. They move to the left. Pennies will cover their eyes & they abandon under the fallen roof the meter gone ticking & nobody there, thick slabs of paint, not one person appearing in the picture. This is her breath his breath awaiting the sculpture of words, the parts of the lesson not yet attended to breathing out shocks of ruby horizon. These leanings gone, finch-finch to cloth

unwoven & she is stranded in current qualities of thought. Qualities of foreboding.)

She was never going back because just before dawn
swallows ascend in accusation, the sound of bottles
glittering the street & the blind lifted at the corner
to look out to clouds coming in with the going out
of darkness. She has no stories of that night to tell
you. The green slivers, the translucent slivers, the silver
underpinnings of stars. In this landscape gone to meet
her small dark horse the secret's paused to touch his
back to touch his coarse mane, wind come undone
& low hills fly by sound. She has no stories, she has
no scored vantage of the person she pretended to be,
wrapped in gold in feathers cover her eyes. There in
the heaviness of location, under lights, the sidewalk
blinds against black grass & they walk two by two
so loud & so large, drowning out the birds. But this
is what she meant by the safety of inside the car as
they go narrowing down the road, sun warming glass
warming thighs as she thinks of his lips & the way the
sun slants across the room in the morning. Not able to
diverge from the call of the bird, crosses hold up thick
wire, talking through lines.

& 17 miles
downriver
nothing but
microbes
survive

(the lake drained
the lake filled)

acid eating away
at the bridge
aluminum
coating over
fish gills

iron
hydroxide
coagulates
staining water
bright orange

carried to
receiving rivers
& spilled
into the
bay (the
swans

the swans)

She was an afternoon bled to the time of what had
been the song was no longer song, the forest no longer
the forest, animals vanished to the cue of bees, to the
river is not just the river but holds legends in relief. The
woman in reeds breathing murky water. The man &
the stone that was starred. Pages begin to disintegrate
& so she puts them into a glass cylinder & buries it
under the holly tree. Come morning there is yelling &
glass breaking & she leaves, walking down to the boat
launch to lean against the sycamore tree. Met with
the imprint of bark, met with boot leather & pocking
the silty ground with her heel. Each sentence paces
out its own rate of composition. Hung in the trees
the lanterns are breathing, the air is breathing this is
evening this is her only life. If not for the river, then
for the river rock & the horse in the field waylaid by
tradition. The question remains & the town is a breath
away. She knows little of it, voices coursing through
air by wood & crystal. By satellite. To the woman in
the black dress & black bonnet she wants to say *Glean
Open* but words form *Green Ocean* because she opens
her eyes & sees a landscape of memory.

Against the alley where we were marked in hound wind as in your love could only
come across when darked, I place our least useful movement in our ends.
                                                        But then,
but there within the lilies the last touch sprang & measured hard, measured live &
adjusted to the street, the startled seer.
                                We had to slow in our fall under the barrel
moon to ugly grasses.
                        & so this contributes to my inclination to take, always, the
turn to the right. Turn-turn & corner clipped was called a circle.
                                                With such acts the
life of record begins: apprehension called to round, & round to hinge in the dark
where the lawn dips out of sight.

& stilled the list of tincture grows & grows. At midnight a half-gale setting our
rushes to wildly swaying & rattling the dead seed heads of our weeds. The rhythms
work into the spine & these are the marks of what fades into questioning, the hour
piercing & plowing deep furrows in the surface of our waters.

Dusk clasped shut &
the river-breath darting

to air hinged inside
my lungs. The daily pressured

the remark woven in

point one, & then, point two
let go in a slip wire-
line. These were the answers

compiled, were beaten
wing one & wing two.

Who lifted me up

small animal through trees.

Time points to the hour of the curtain, the glass swan still warm
                                        from the
                                        child's hand
                                        the room
become a minor legacy as this telling frosts over double-paned glass:
the road one way & the cold seeped into the papery fronds of
                                        the fern.
Camera lens approximating the landscape's gaze, the locket lost &
                                        the bees
                                        died out
to a crack in weather composing the back of the mirror. & so paused
with a sprig of dried sage. Paused, we wait for pears to shake down
                                        from the
                                        sky,
                                        the new-
limbed tree bent in heaviness, this moment giving in to the pull where
                                        sigh acts
                                        as talisman
against the red storm gathering history's compression. Narrated in dust
the distance holds a steeple to the right here garnered, here collided
                                        with the
                                        press of
geese V'ed, vented breeze, verse torqued to fit on its side & bathed in
afternoon light as snow comes to settle in the joints of white stairs.

Yesterday insists on questions of interval, power, but here she stands thinking about warmth, a new context in which to register damp air, sage grasses appearing & disappearing outside the window. The sun came up & everything grayed. The sun went down & all that was caught fire, curled into clay. Attention now turned to the home inside her mind, the back barn burnt to the ground the day before yesterday. How the flames roared. How the children pointed & she was miles & miles from there. These are imprints of events sketched in the imagination of memory. & he is the yellow tinge atop the trees, opening his arms wide, telling the world to go to hell then talking of the river & its rebirth out of pollution, purified to a better self. A succession of days offers lessons in humility, grace, grief as the mother's phone rings & rings but ensconced in her chair she no longer rises to receive it. Hinged & writing of clay & trees & canvas & glass & people aflame with the world turning on its side to good night & morning was so very long ago, geese waking to a sky wrestling its dark.

Against the hound wind of I miss you in your flower-file, out of the doors of the great room out to the patio, out to the sea.

                    If I miss you in hindsight I'll indulge myself by naming you just one in a succession of the fragile-shouldered.

                                  This in place of the leaves did not stay long this year, mashed down in a projection of winter.

      This in place of I wait for the mosaic of ice, for what's spiked into purpose, bent to the tincture of rooms. & the leaf did sing out with rot & rot, my voice tilling regardless.

They call this the final season's evolution of weather: wind roaring down from the hills over forests of oak & beech & hickory & pine. It blew us east, towards the sea two hundred miles away where beheld in illumination we come apart, a series of cut blossoms.

The notion of revision
of turning back

to midnight molded
by patches of
vine seeping &

the red oak relinquishing its brilliancy.

Important:
what has come before
now hot in the mind

& so waiting along the river

for the thread pulling out-out-out—

Become Tree, Become Bird

"Then the juniper tree began to move. The branches moved apart, then moved together again, just as if someone were rejoicing & clapping his hands. At the same time a mist seemed to rise from the tree, & in the center of this mist it burned like a fire, & a beautiful bird flew out of the fire singing magnificently, & it flew high into the air, & when it was gone, the juniper tree was just as it had been before & the cloth with the bones was no longer there. Marlene, however, was as happy & contented as if her brother were still alive. & she went merrily into the house, sat down at the table, & ate. Then the bird flew away & lit on a goldsmith's house, & began to sing."

Jacob & Wilhelm Grimm, *The Juniper Tree*

Down bird
down sky
down jet-
jet whirring

covered in birds
I saw salt.
I saw with eyes
of salt hard by
the herd
wading shallows

like the tilling moon
rose & set
& rose
out of long grass
to cure the sky
struck in
vapor trails.

No nest here.
No downy feather.
No bed.
No rest.

On the wall
the sun drawing
paths & somehow
the middle of
the day spans

hours. Land & weather submerge. In the Grimms' version of *The Juniper
Tree* the first wife dies giving birth to a little son as red as blood as white
as snow, the second wife bears a daughter. The smoke in the field divides

the sea from
called to the
sea, land from

the harrowed. & when the second wife looked at her daughter she loved
her very much but then she looked at the little boy & it pierced her heart.

The dog barks
& a choir of
geese mark the

hunting season, the turn-turn, the nape of your neck as you said *lilac*—
chosen in the hothouse interior of her rooms with the gesture of a well.
She thought he would stand in her way & was always thinking about
how she could get the entire inheritance for her daughter. This discord

saturates with
the seen-
through-a-glass

with the wait-in-the doorway-until-you-recognize your name is only a
problem under the distance of certain systems. & the Evil One filled her

mind with this until she grew very angry with the little boy & pushed him
from one corner to the other, constituting, reconstituting, the barn sinking
back into aspen, leaves gone to mulch as light shines on the boy walking

down the sidewalk

singing *Marlene,*

Marlene, an attempt

as in my eyes settle on lupine & sage, ocean & field. & she slapped him here
& cuffed him there until the poor child was always afraid. But if I am in
& through the window & the winter storm walking through blossom-

bare lilac

to crouch

under the

holly tree

departure composing the view from the dock drawn in nettle & air. & he
could never find any peace. Inside the shelter of my body we fall, particles

of sand & salt

among water-

vented pollen

dispersed by

image & breeze.

Went the valley.
Went the swallows* like

weather torn & densed
into shell, matched
by shifts* in the text, gaps fused

by detonation of eye
to eye to light
lost & day lost
& time—we whisper

this—drawn*
to the edge of its measure. Meteor.

* Before the tale begins the character appears at the window in a robe stitched with peacock eyes. She composes a story on top of other stories. Facets shine off snow.

* The years spanning the end of childhood through adolescence, she tells the frost, were courtyard & winter apple.

* Sun applies pressure to the blind to the lamppost with its globe swanning out. Come noon, the blue tint of field saturate with light with the radio, pouring.

To stay the impact we bred
the so-sweet of leaf
rot & tincture*—tincture

pressed into word.
As such I leave behind*

remnants of typesetter's lead, cordite, a flash
gone off laying the lamb bare
to her hiding. Birds stall in suspension

as if struck* through with wiring.

* The years spanning the end of adolescence to the
present, she says to the birds, were a paring knife, a drop
of blood on snow.

* Announced by hard soles on wood floors he enters the
room & she imagines herself running through the ice &
the blue.

* At the edge of the field she twists into juniper.

If dust folded*
to syllable—if packed

against mineral deposits, time
subsisting as a hand a
willow, a swallow ordering

uncircumscribed* burn. The bird
marks a gesture of spirit above our heads

before diving down feather
& flesh, sinew & bone turned
all at once to stone.*

* Touching her elbow he calls her back without uttering a sound.

* The future, she thinks, resting forehead to glass, is the relation of goldsmith to chain, cobbler to shoe, mill worker to millstone.

* The room fills with their breathing, seascape lashing its frame above the piano, paperweight swan a prism.

Shadow: Waking in the middle of the smoldering field, guitar on my lap like the baby I never. & I was your Dietrich, your Gretchen, your Philomena, your Marlene. That night, the tree again in flame. & then the field.

Source: As Orrin W. Robinson points out in *Grimm Language: Grammar, Gender, & Genuineness in the Fairy Tales*, it has been long recognized that, despite the penchant of early 19th-century Europe for pure national forms, the Brothers Grimm did not arrive at their collection by slogging through the fields, woods, & villages of German-speaking Europe, eliciting age-old folktales from peasant farmers.

She becomes an attempt, eyes settled on a field.

Shadow: Your hair smelled of smoke & ash & I have not forgotten departure sketched on thin paper: our son replaced with a child's drawing of a bird, our house replaced by a paper square.

Source: The sources used by the Brothers Grimm were demonstrably literary & many of their tales are not exclusively German. From the 1812 edition on, one way the Grimms made their fairy tales seem authentically German was to render them in some form of dialect. While in only 21 of the 211 tales do we find the body-text (as opposed to poems or quotes) in any kind of dialect, 10% is enough, perhaps, to lend vernacular weight to the Germanicity of the collection.

For the cross-hatched: a small hurt.

Out to the greenhouse shears in hand to rush the orange in & what warms through plastic sheeting & glass. To hold this in mind while cutting rosebuds, iris.

A literary work, once it has arisen, no longer changes.

& secret, this glimpse of fence & white sky infused with the sound of the peacock nesting in the horse's stall.

Two mock suns rose with the sun, followed it all through the day.

& it exists only when two agents are present: the author & the reader. The mediating link between them is a book, manuscript, or poem.

A topography of shale—clay & quartz & calcite slowly harden, foliated compaction & a propensity to split easily along layers.

What's written cannot be unwritten & so a literary work is immutable, but the reader always changes. Aristotle was read by the ancient Greeks, the Arabs, & the Humanists, & we read him too, but all read & understand him differently.

(My mother, sang the bird, she killed me)

Every reader will have noticed that two color fields juxtaposed without separation will, when viewed from some distance, appear in the border region to flow into each other. But then to wake in one's bed, to open the curtain, make coffee, shower, dress. As if the day could be ordinary after all night breathing ash.

This experience is best exemplified when viewing mosaic images or woven tapestries where mixture is obtained from isolated points or lines. I am & am not the woman in reeds breathing murky water. You are & are not the man & the stone that was starred.

Whether this appearance of fusion is the result of the intervening air layer or of rays coming from different colors crossing each other in the eye is a matter beyond us. For if meaning manifests through sensation, let me touch the letterforms. Text become a fallen tree, the split place of its purpled heart.

Bluing through
the river of
the book,
feathers cover
my eyes. One day the woman had gone upstairs to her room when her
little daughter came up, the sound of wet leaves drawing day through
parched grass & said mother, give me an apple. A lit moth marking its
source on
the map
where the
inevitability
of faith
gives over to a matchstick & the little cracked cup. Yes my child said
the woman & gave her a beautiful apple out of the chest, air become
land grown
granite-heavy
& plinth. The chest had a heavy lid with a large sharp iron lock & here
the river
wides &
slows, wind
shifts through
rue anemone on the ridge as a bleating called force pries in. Mother, said
Marlene, is brother not to have one too? As the field washes away, hills

                                        bone & the
                                        mind bone,
bank split apart by autumn crocus & meadow rose. This made the
woman angry but she said yes when he comes home from school.
                                        Air become
                                        dove. When
from the window she saw him coming home it was as though the Evil
One came over her. Take my hand. She grabbed the apple & took it
away from her daughter saying you shall not have one before your
brother. These patterns construct my frequent thoughts where the
                                        river pools
                                        under maples
                                        each year
                                        leafing to
                                        darker
                                        crimson &
                                        I write
                                        the names
                                        of flowers
                                        connoting the
                                        island burns.

True readers always read creatively. Put a penny in the vase. Put a tablet of aspirin, distilled water preserving the lily until it opens.

In the atmosphere ice crystals act as prisms, light rays refracting mock suns—sundogs—through the diamond dust.

A work of literature can bring such readers joy, inspire them, or fill them with indignation. They may wish to interfere in the heroes' fortunes, reward or punish them, change their tragic fate to a happy one, put a triumphant villain to death.

Red-colored at the side nearest the sun, farther out colors grade through orange to blue then merge with the white of the sun's halo.

But when heat comes it doesn't matter how quickly you plunge the stems. With such acts the life of the story folds in.

Called to round & hinge in the dark, the vase smashed on the flagstone as I startled.

But readers, no matter how deeply aroused by a work of literature, are unable & are not allowed to introduce any changes to suit their own tastes or the views of their age.

(My father, sang the bird, he ate me)

This flowing together is itself the cause of intermediary colors. It is easy to see this when viewing a blue field juxtaposed with a yellow one, for a green border area will appear along the edge. You read within these valley-folds the collision of North America with Africa; I read within the tree a woman singing.

When juxtaposing green & red, gray will appear at the borderline. This is most clearly apparent if the two color fields are inclined toward each other at an angle so that one color reflects onto the other. Suppose she had left before cutting her finger on the paring knife. Packed her suitcase. Thrown on her hat & coat to slip out the door before he came home. What happens to the story then?

In a garment made of green & red shot fabric (cangiante) where the illuminated areas appear red & those in the shade green, an illuminated crease will produce a gray reflection. No apple, no son, no second wife. She worries the clock, the forest, the glass swan clutched in the child's hand.

marking
the bloom
inside
the juniper
an evergreen

(this need
gone bled
through
lace by the
sparrow)

white gloves
& pliers
we stuffed
the trees
to still
the rains

juniper from
the Latin
iuniperis
the morning
found altered
a state
of rose
iuniperis
youth-renewing

from
iuvenis
(young) &
parere (to
produce)

these Latin
roots yield
the English
juvenile &
parent

twice-
answered
with always
the same
bright
measure in
the sky kept
closed (the

alley is
the only
way
between
the bird
& the
bird)

Shadow: From within a shell of silence I first heard the violin, which began while standing on the pier & you were running your hand up my dress & we didn't care who saw, not the men with their still-flopping fish, not the boy's mother struggling with his kite.

Source: The Grimm's source for tale number 47, *Von dem Machandelboom, (The Juniper Tree)*, recorded in the wonderfully simple, but poetic, Low German dialect, was the German Romantic painter, Philipp Otto Runge (1777–1810). Runge's tale was first published in Achim von Arnim's *Journal for Hermits (Zeitung für Einsiedler)* in 1809.

Touching carved into scales of light.

Shadow: Rebar, concrete, rock, bone: hard things making mulch of the earth with their sinking. & what if I were to sink. & how then are you to find me, I thought, standing in the burnt-through field with the horse, his ribs sharp under a patchy chestnut coat. This is breath, I thought, memory of the pier fading, sunlight slashed off mercury fading. Then the rhythm of air forced out of moist nostrils, animal pressed.

Source: The tale was certainly well-known in German-speaking cultures long before Runge & the Grimms wrote it down. For example, beginning with the earliest versions of *Faust* (1774), Goethe has his Gretchen sing a variation of the bird's song in prison, strangely appropriating the voice of her murdered child as her own.

But then the violin became waves lashing as the red barn burned back into its field.

She threw
the apple
into the
chest & shut it, a century burnt across eyes. Then the little boy came
in & the Evil One made her say to him kindly my son do you want
an apple.
As our will
disintegrates
into secrets
said to shallowed stone the fire dies. & she looked at him fiercely. The
willowed
island parts
the river
abandoned
in the mulch of the banks, the arum lily become sails drawn up,
a white ship in a white sea. Mother, said the little boy, how angry
you look, yes, give me an apple. Knotted, grown every which-way
& winning
over gravity
icy branches
extend the
flow of ever-
occurring words, hands, eyes lifted over power lines. Then it seemed
to her as if she had to persuade him. Come with me she said opening
the lid of the chest, take out an apple for yourself. The road to the steel-

                                        pivoted bridge
                                        half-anchors
                                        in demi-release,
in memory, eyes closed to the swans on the banks of the frozen lake &
while the little boy was leaning over, the Evil One prompted her &
crash! she slammed down the lid & his head flew off falling among
                                        the apples.
                                        The lake
                                        heated &
                                        drained
                                        without
                                        question in
the manner sentiment welds to regret. Then fear overcame her & she
thought perhaps I can absolve myself of this. We're asked to the cut
pouring known to some as God. So she went upstairs to her room
to her chest of drawers & took a white scarf from the top drawer.
                                        Manifest in
                                        battering my
                                        body's warm
center is a consequence of yellow light blooming after the rain stopped
                                        & I saw you
                                        afraid. & set
his head on his neck again, tying the scarf around it so no wound could
be seen. Then she set him on a chair in front of the door & put the apple
                                        in his hand.

Cangiante, a term derived from the Italian *cangiare* (to change) is characterized by the painter's changing to a different, lighter hue when the original hue cannot be made light enough. Or, on the converse, changing to a darker hue when the original hue cannot be made dark enough. The offering of an apple.

When painting shadows on a yellow object, the painter may change, for example, from the color yellow to the color red regardless of the object's actual color simply because the yellow he has to work with cannot be made dark enough to render shadows. Tonight you are like Momus blaming Vulcan for not placing a window in the breast of each man by which whatever was felt or thought might easily have been seen. We spend the rest of the night in silence.

The greatest practitioner of this technique was Michelangelo & it is illustrated in many parts of the Sistine Chapel ceiling. In this landscape gone to meet her small dark horse the secret's paused to touch his back to touch his coarse mane with a prayer to the sky as the wind comes undone & low hills fly by sound.

Folklore also presupposes two agents, but different agents, namely, the performer & the listener, initially opposing each other directly, without a mediating link.
                                                                                                    They
attributed the week of mock suns to the weather system but to myself I said socket holding & I had never felt so sexual, nubs of flowers pressed underneath winter-slick bark.
                            & the little sigh of waves slapping & unable to decipher the omen. Perihelion, phantom sun, mock sun, too much light in the eyes.
                                                                        As a rule,
performers' works are not created by them, they are reciters of others' works, listeners becoming producers by interweaving texts.
                                                        The large plastic swans having
been stored in the boathouse, map run through with manmade lakes.

Methods of production include addition, subtraction, rearrangement, juxtaposition, & graft. They are figures specific to folklore, & all of them—from the primitive chorus to the folktale narrator—deserve our closest attention.

(My sister, sang the bird, Marlene)

To love gone stark,
the page gone stark
in silver permeates* river, geese,
& snow. We were

two questions & folded in half & applied
to the long lantern cast.
To the forced blue wiring*
pent to the dove

to under hoof & hoof—hard soles
cannot mar this heavy varnish—my written*
in bales. In critique of splinter we skin against.

* Chosen in the possibility of she will go & he will stay,
an opposition of waiting as mercury pooled in her palm
knows no motion so long as the hand's held flat. A
month went by, & the snow was gone.

* & two months, & everything was green. & three
months, & all the flowers came out of the earth.

* This thought is a process as is oxygen emanating from
juniper & ash grown to encompass the black & white
film where picadors circle the bull. Under such direction
she feels like water culverted & fed into an artificial lake.
Complete with swans.

So we hinged like weather
entering dark* vowels, hollow

cupping echo* cupping
hollow. As such summer's lily-wrung

until the stopper's out.
The window directs*

all my looking towards
the red pulsed-pull & weed.

* & four months & all the trees in the woods grew
thicker, their branches entwined.

* & the birds sang until the woods resounded & blossoms
fell from the trees.

* Then the fifth month passed & she stood beneath the
juniper tree which smelled so sweet that she fell on her
knees.

Then folded into circumference
I am marked* sitting here

punctuating the said* caught
in the flick of his head,
flick of his mane. Juniper unraveling

the far corner
of the field. Such possibility*

fraught in the blue-green tufts. Acred.

* In slow motion, the bull bowed down & after the seventh month she picked the juniper berries & ate them greedily. Then she grew sick & sorrowful.

* Then, the sword drawn through. Swans pulling through water two by two.

* The eighth month passed & she called her husband to her & cried & said if I die, then bury me beneath the juniper tree. Circling the field bathed in low winter light what is the interior weather of a tale?

Shadow: To consider oneself to be purely a body facing another body. & then fingers run over the floral border of the quilt so as to touch the long-dead hands that once knotted pink into tulips, emerald & sage into leaf, vine, lattice. My fingers along this edge until I come to a bare place where the stitches had been ripped. Music: the strung-glass ornaments of constellation. Jittery.

Source: Runge was born into a family of German-speaking shipbuilders in Wolgast, West Pomerania, then under Swedish rule. As a sickly child, he often missed school & at an early age learned the art of scissor-cut silhouettes from his mother, practicing them throughout his life.

She was there by the side of the road, a ghost with blooms in her spine.

Shadow: I was on the path when it happened. First I thought a stunning fog so thick it blacked half the bridge opposite. & never did the remaining cables look so delicate. Then, the billow creeping slowly toward me & I knew before I thought: twisted tramcars & bones. To become the last place touched by fire. To put your hand on the horse's ribs. To with your last force push in at his heart.

Source: In 1801 Runge moved to Dresden where meeting Caspar David Friedrich, among others, augmented his official artistic training. He began extensive study of the writings of Jakob Boehme & on a visit to Weimar in 1803 he unexpectedly met Goethe & the two formed a life-long friendship based on common interests in color & art.

What remains in excess of narrative folds.

We come here
bare or wrapped
in linen the
moment held
in our bones as
ash-light falls

over the worried edge of water meeting sky. After this Marlene came
into the kitchen to her mother who was standing by the fire with a pot
of hot water before her, which she was stirring around & around. Slow

& strange
we're pulled
south through

blurred streets. Mother, said Marlene, brother is sitting at the door & he
looks totally white & has an apple in his hand & I asked him to give me
the apple but he did not answer me & I am afraid. Getting out of our car

to wander the
metal & salt
of accident

& shore. Go back to him said her mother & if he will not answer you
box his ears. Wrapped in blankets & rough sheets, mirror-warped to
I've seen between myself & myself, the writing stitched into eiderdown. So
Marlene went to him & said brother give me the apple but he was silent,

bees filling

air. So she hit him on the ear & his head fell off &, terrified, Marlene
began crying & screaming & ran to her mother & said oh mother I have

knocked my brother's head off. & crying & crying she could not be
                                        comforted.
                                        & there I
                                        blanched into
                                        aspen & window-
                                        split light an
afternoon V mosaic-worked into garlands of orange roses rewriting
                                        the planetree,
                                        the hush, bird
                                        egg cradled in
the hollow of my hand. Marlene, said the mother, what have you done,
be quiet, said the mother, & don't let anyone know about this. Siren-
called waves & blank forehead of asking the question to the bolt of a
                                        picture a red
                                        horse sunk
                                        deep into
                                        deeper red
as the earth was red there. No-no-no you cannot tell anyone my daughter
                                        for this crime
                                        you have
                                        committed
                                        cannot be
                                        undone.

In the image of the prophet Daniel, for instance, the use of cangiante can be clearly seen in the transition from green to yellow in the Prophet's robes. Our conversation depends on the telling of the tale, paper apple & paper knife yielding no blood, the paper boy no sorrow as he lifts away, loose leaf on wind.

After Michelangelo's time, the technique found widespread acceptance & is now a standard painting technique. You insist that if the character leaves the narrative she will have no stories beyond those of the person she pretended to be, wrapped in gold in feathers cover her eyes.

Here, the reference is to a colored surface reflecting light onto another surface of a different color. The appearance of the second surface changes as a result of the spectral composition of light falling on it & being reflected. Not able to diverge from the call of the bird, crosses hold up thick wire, the sound of talking through lines.

are we
mistaken if we
find Kronos
in the
river in the
father devouring
his children

fidelity
to the golden
chain the
stone the
red leather
shoes

(I made
a little
winter
sun &
dropped it
there)

if we
see in the
boy-bird-soul
Philomena
raped by her
brother-in-

law & they
cut out
her
tongue

but
nevertheless
the bird
sings out
nevertheless
she wove
her story
into a
tapestry

the unspoken
overlooking
the field

& the juniper
grown
interior
grown

nerved

Performers do not repeat their texts word for word but introduce changes into them.

    To sink slowly into slow moving waters into lakes, lagoons, river deltas, floodplains. With leaves & small sea creatures to sediment into rock.

                                         Or as a
preservative, mixing equal parts lemonade to water & a drop of bleach. For roses, add a teaspoon of sugar or a can of 7 Up.

                         To hold what flashed rare like the *Sun Dog Painting*—the *Vädersolstavlan*—depicting two hours in the morning of April 20, 1535 when the skies over Stockholm filled with multiple white circles & arcs while additional suns appeared around the sun.

                              Thought to be a message from God.

    A low sound at the edge of the field felt in my chest. Marked by barbed wire, by reaching through to pull the crocus & forsythia nevertheless.

Even if these changes are insignificant (but they can be very great), even if the changes that take place in folklore texts are sometimes as slow as geological processes, what is important is the fact of changeability of folklore compared with the stability of literature.

(Gathered all my bones, sang the bird)

Because gray, placed between red & green, is without individuality, but rather exists as the general dissolution of opposing forces, harmony in this case is already implicit in the quarrel between two opposing colors. Though their seeds contain cyanide, it is unnecessary to core apples before feeding them to birds. She parses the fruit & yields a dispensation of suns recovered in the form of little stars.

However, the green transition color between blue & yellow, having a different individuality, disturbs the effect of blue as well as of yellow, because both their individuality is fully consumed in their product. Of premonition you say: had she known what will happen to the son it is hard to believe she would have stayed. Present to knowledge but absent of choice, I counter, she creates a way to remain.

A certain agitation necessarily appears in the two pure colors because green (the result combined of full force action of blue & yellow) is not perceived in a determined manner. The agitation in this combination is, in truth, a dissonance, but it can be eliminated with the placement of an intermediate color. Attention now turned to the home inside her mind, the back barn burnt to the ground the day before yesterday.

Shadow: Silence surrounded the horse & I stood near him, the rest of town submerged in soft baying & continuous digging machines. No space from which to pry myself from the world around me, its ash & corpses, inorganic, organic, animal, human, vegetal—indistinguishable, all.

Source: At the beginning of the Napoleonic wars Runge & his wife moved back to his parental home in West Pomerania, & then to Hamburg. In 1807 Runge developed the concept of the color sphere. In 1809 he intensified his work on color & published written versions of two local, West Pomeranian fairy tales, *The Fisherman & His Wife* & *The Juniper Tree*. The body-texts of both works employ the Low German dialect Plattdeutsch from his native region.

The struggle of mountains under shrouds of snow.

Shadow: Memory slowing the sun in its going down, flanked by mock suns until just before sunset. & then: release. In another scenario we might try to save the characters by accelerating the season: flowers come out of earth & trees thicken & the juniper bears no mark of fire.

Source: A mathematical model of philosophical reflections on color, Runge's color sphere develops from the tenant that there are only three colors: red, yellow, & blue. His goal was to establish the complete world of possible colors & their relations from the mixture of only five pure source elements: red, yellow, blue, black, & white. Encouraged by Goethe he wrote *Farben-Kugle (Color-Sphere)*, an 1810 text detailing his work on the relationship of colors.

The music come out of my mouth tipped on a tongue of arrows.

Then the mother
took the little boy's
body & chopped
it into pieces
putting them into a pot & cooking him into a stew. Bathed in the yellow
light of the kitchen Marlene stood watching & crying & all her tears fell
into the pot. Narrated in dust the distance holds a steeple to the right here
garnered, here
collided with
the press of
geese V'ed
vented breeze, yesterday's salt visible to the lens. Then the father came
home & sat at the table & said where is my son? Our moment giving in
to the pull
where sigh
acts as talisman
against the red storm gathering. & the mother served up a large dish of
stew & Marlene could not stop crying. Here we wait for pears to shake
down from the sky the new-limbed tree bent in heaviness. Then the
father said
again where is
my son? Paused & yet at the same time leaving with the tincture moon,
oh said the mother he has gone across the country to his mother's great-
uncle he will stay there awhile. The lamb lost & you, humming under
your breath to the metronome of the clock's tick, a crack in the weather

                                                  composing
                                                  the back
                                                  of the mirror.
                                                  I am unhappy,
said the man, that he did not even say good-bye to me, oh my son. &
the mother ladled more stew into his bowl & he ate. The locket lost &
                                                  the plummeting
                                                  beyond doubt.
                                                  Marlene cried
                                                  & could not stop
crying & as the father ate he threw the bones under the table & on the
table the glass swan still warm from the child's hand. Marlene ran
upstairs to her chest of drawers & took her best silk scarf from the
bottom & gathered all the bones from beneath the table & tied them
up in the scarf & carried them out to lay them in the garden underneath
                                                  the juniper tree,
                                                  cold seeping
into the papery fronds of the fern. & after she placed them there she
suddenly felt better & her tears began to dry a trace of salt & silver down
her cheeks. Then a mist of bees rose from the juniper & the tree began
to move, branches bursting into sparks as a flock of sparrows flew
                                                  out. & then
                                                  the tree,
                                                  tremoring,
                                                  was just as
                                                  it had been.

Our current preoccupation with remnant: shredding papers that avoided fire, air gone pure with electricity, cats nesting in the wooden box lined with scraps.

If the reader of a work of literature is powerless, anyone listening to folklore is a potential future performer who, in turn, consciously or unconsciously, will introduce changes into the work.

Some gas is held in shale's natural fractures, some in pore spaces, some absorbed in organic material.

In the mind's eye the drape draws back on the stubble field & geese picking through ice.

Perihelia in Rome, summer of 1629, prompt Descartes to write *Le Monde*, a work of natural philosophy that he withholds from the public upon hearing of Galileo's condemnation.

Too much light in the eyes.

Everything out-of-date & incongruous with new attitudes, tastes, & ideology will be discarded. Sentences lost in berry, seedcone, needle-leaf.

(Tied them in a silken handkerchief, sang the bird)

In the past this kind of disharmonic combination was used whenever the eye was to be stimulated & made attentive, rather than pleased, for example, in uniforms, flags, coats of arms, playing cards, etc. She knows that if she stays there'll be erring in the branches, breath held against the broken windows of the solarium.

Consider the following facts: all those colors which, when mixed, dissolve into gray, produce lively & harmonic contrasts; pure colors in their juxtaposition stimulate the eye as a dissonance. In answer to impossible questions I borrow the story of bones burned & the heart of the tree opened to the heart of the bird.

In consequence, it is imaginable that a select combination of brilliant colors, without a need for interrupting their sequence with gray, is capable of enhancing the significance of, & impression created by, a work of art, just as musical sounds can do so for the sense & spirit of a poem. The sun came up & the field tendered to green. The sun went down & all that was green caught fire, curled into clay, leaves & branches russetting.

iuniperis: now flower now
seed, late snow

fallen & in the aftermath
the tree dug up

by its roots, branches cut
& then bundled

as the bird surged up
& away. We wait for night

a strip torn from my dress

to wrap the needle-yew.
To incite the burn.

iuniperis: match struck
to branch, field

receding house receding &
they could not catch us

a-run along
the river. Flambeaux—

smoke billow—
a little clue of light
released low & blue

after having been pressed
so long

to the vortex of a shell.

To attend decay as it sets in: bitter rotted stems & heavy heads. Or, to snip the bloom before it browns.

Gas in shale fractures is produced immediately. Gas absorbed into organic material releases as the formation pressure is drawn down by the well.

Force open the rose, press it between the pages of the book next to fragments of lichen & fern.

We can predict the forms mock suns would take on other planets: on Jupiter, Saturn, Uranus, & Neptune clouds of ammonia & methane could regularly produce a veritable *Vädersolstavlan*—alien skies filled with multiple halos revolving four or more suns.

The green slivers, the translucent slivers, the silver underpinning of stars.

A work of folklore exists in constant flux & cannot be studied in depth if it is recorded only once; it should be recorded as many times as possible.

(Laid them beneath the juniper tree, sang the bird)

(Sang the bird *tweet tweet tweet* what a beautiful bird am I)

iuniperis: harvested &
yielding wood ash spread

beneath the new-
budded apple. The sky

assumes the debt
of the breath-lent field

coming just now to green

in the absence
of juniper & ice.

Sources:

Along with a debt to physical landscape, this book is indebted to many texts. Fragments & transformations of the following works appear above & below the surfaces of this book—

"Art as Device." Viktor Shklovsky translated by Benjamin Sher. Dalkey Archive Press, 1991
Blue Studios. Rachel Blau Duplessis. University of Alabama Press, 2006
"Come Away from Her." Intaglio with hand-applied watercolor. Kiki Smith, 2003
Grimm Language: Grammar, Gender, & Genuineness in the Fairy Tales. Orrin W. Robinson. John Benjamins Publishing Company, 2010
Gender in the Mirror: Cultural Imagery and Women's Agency. Diana Tietjens Meyers. Oxford University Press, 2002
HERmione. H.D. New Directions, 1981
"In Bloom." Acrylic and oil on canvas. Zsolt Bodoni, 2012
Landscape and Memory. Simon Schama. Vintage, 1996
On the Problem of Empathy. Edith Stein translated by Waltraut Stein. Institute for Carmelite Studies, 1989
Philipp Otto Runge's Color Sphere. Philipp Otto Runge edited and translated by Rolf G. Kuehni. Inter-Society Color Council, 2008
The Annotated Brothers Grimm. Jackob and Wilhelm Grimm edited by Maria Tatar. W.W. Norton, 2004
"The Juniper Tree" from *The Grimm Brothers' Childrens' and Household Tales*. Compiled, translated and classified by D.L. Ashliman, 1998-2011
"The Juniper Tree: A Study of a Tale from Grimm." Ernest Parkin. Edgeways Books, 2003
The Juniper Tree, an opera in two acts. Philip Glass and Robert Moran; libretto by Arthur Yorinks, 1984
The Juniper Tree. Film. Nietzchka Keene, 1990
The Waves. Virginia Woolf. Harvest Books, 1978
Theory and History of Folklore. Vladimir Propp translated by Ariadna Martin and Richard P. Martin. University of Minnesota Press, 1984
Three. Ann Quin. Dalkey Archive Press, 2001
Time in Feminist Phenomenology. Edited by Christina Schües, Dorothea Olkowski, and Helen A. Fielding. Indiana University Press, 2011
"Touch." Set of six etchings with aquatint and drypoint. Kiki Smith, 2006
Touching Feeling: Affect, Pedagogy, Performativity. Eve Sedgwick. Duke University Press, 2003
Transparent Minds. Dorrit Cohn. Princeton University Press, 1978
Under the Sea Wind. Rachel Carson. Penguin, 1991

Internet searches for "abandoned mine drainage" "cangiante" "foliate" "gas well drilling" "juniper" "Old Forge borehole" "parahelion" "Philipp Otto Runge" "preserving cut flowers" "shale" "Vädersolstavlan"

ACKNOWLEDGMENTS:

Poems from this book have appeared in the following journals & anthologies, often under different titles & in different configurations: *The Arcadia Project: North American Postmodern Pastoral, Cab/Net, The Chicago Review, The Colorado Review, Conjunctions, Crazy Horse, Interim, Lit, New American Writing, The Sonora Review, Wildlife, Xantippe, 1913: A Journal of Forms*. Many thanks to the editors of these projects.

Susquehanna University's faculty research grants & sabbatical leave were indispensable to the generation & completion of this work. Thank you to the University for supporting this book.

Thank you to my family & friends for their encouragement. Thank you Molly Bendall, Forrest Gander, Aaron McCollough, Donna Stonecipher, & Robert Strong for reading & commenting on various drafts of this book. Special appreciation to G.C. Waldrep, for your belief in the manuscript & for the concept of a double-book. Deep gratitude to Omnidawn, particularly Rusty Morrison, for your editorial insight. Thank you, Ashley Lamb, for *Moss*. To Mark Szybist, for the secret river—thank you.

Photo Credit: Mark Szybist

Karla Kelsey's first book, *Knowledge, Forms, the Aviary* was selected by Carolyn Forché for the 2005 Ahsahta Press Sawtooth Poetry Prize. *Iteration Nets*, her second book, was published by Ahsahta in 2010. She edits & writes for *The Constant Critic*, &, with Aaron McCollough, co-directs SplitLevel Texts. A graduate of UCLA, the Iowa Writer's Workshop, & the University of Denver, Karla is a recipient of a Fulbright lectureship. She has taught creative writing & American literature at the Eötvös Loránd University & at the Eötvös Collegium, both in Budapest, & specializes in poetry at Susquehanna University.

A Conjoined Book
by Karla Kelsey

Cover text set in Warnock Pro, Cochin LT Std, & Adobe Garamond Pro.
Interior text set in Adobe Garamond Pro.

Cover art by Ashley Lamb: *Moss*, collage, 9.5" x 7.5," 2013.
(http://ashleyklamb.com/)
&
Black seamless pattern, vector silhouette
by Natykach Nataliia/Shutterstock

Cover & interior design by Cassandra Smith

Offset printed in the United States
by Edwards Brothers Malloy, Ann Arbor, Michigan
on 55# Enviro Natural 100% Recycled 100% PCW
Acid Free Archival Quality FSC Certified Paper
with Rainbow FSC Certified Colored End Papers

Omnidawn Publishing
Richmond, California
2014

Rusty Morrison & Ken Keegan, Senior Editors & Publishers
Cassandra Smith, Poetry Editor & Book Designer
Gillian Hamel, Poetry Editor & OmniVerse Managing Editor
Sara Mumolo, Poetry Editor
Peter Burghardt, Poetry Editor & Book Designer
Turner Canty, Poetry Editor
Liza Flum, Poetry Editor & Social Media
Sharon Osmond, Poetry Editor & Bookstore Outreach
Juliana Paslay, Fiction Editor & Bookstore Outreach Manager
Gail Aronson, Fiction Editor
RJ Ingram, Social Media
Pepper Luboff, Feature Writer
Craig Santos Perez, Media Consultant